The Quick Guide of Awesomeness:

An easy way to jump-start your business or company.

Gabriel Ronkai

Copyright © 2018 Gabriel Ronkai

All rights reserved.

ISBN-13: 978-1986882927

ISBN-10: 1986882926

CONTENTS

i : Foreword
1: The Five books you must read.
2: The easiest thing to do.
3: What is the biggest problem a business faces?
4: These are four people who could save your company.
5: The best resource sites for businesses.
6: People to follow and listen to.
7: How the 80/20 rule applies to your company.
8: Sales
9: Customer Service
10: Fire prevention
11: FIVE things a CEO must know when you hire them.
12: Resume
13: Perspective
14: CEO
15: Growth
16: Equality in the workplace.
17: Authenticity
18: A me-centric universe.
19: A Teaching Guide.

Foreword

This book was put together to help business owners and CEOs.
The simplicity of the book do not full you. The information here is worth gold.

The Five books you must read.

1. Think and Grow Rich by Napoleon Hill -(because you always start with you)
2. The 7 Habits of Highly Effective People by Stephen Covey
3. The 80/20 Principle: The Secret to Achieving More with Less by Richard Koch
4. The Power of Myth by Joseph Campbell
5. Reality in Advertising by Rosser Reeves

The easiest thing to do.

Believe it or not, the easiest thing to do to fix a problem (if you cannot figure it out in the company) is to bring in an expert.

The bigger consulting firm – the bigger brand name does not mean better quality solution. Usually, it is actually the opposite.

My suggestion is to bring in highly qualified individual experts. You will get a lot better-personalized help.

Why do people running businesses and corporations not bring in expert?

Cost can be a problem. However in my experience most of the time it is because of ego, pride, vanity, and simply not being aware.

What is the biggest problem a business faces?

In my experience, the biggest problems for any business small or large come from NOT knowing their numbers.

More precisely: not knowing variable and fixed costs.

Many companies fail because these costs run away. Your accounting department has to nail down all of the costs to the last cent, and have to know why certain expenses keep going up when there is no apparent reason for it.

Finances for a better term are like cancer. If you do not know what is going on internally it will eventually kill you. However preventative measures can catch things early enough to save your business life.

Unfortunately, most companies are never due preventative maintenance. They just are trying to put out fires.

These are four people who could save your company.

One of the things I learned from my mentor was that there are always people who know more or are better at certain than you.

So these are five people I would always have on a retainer a person running accompany. These people would come in either once a month to check how things are and if things are off somewhere help you to correct them. Or whenever you start a project they would come in to give a direction to which way to go and would check in periodically to make sure everything is going smoothly.

1. A Financial Efficiency expert – You always need to know how your finances are.
2. A Marketing – Brand expert - You need somebody that has knowledge of multiple industries.
3. A Social Media expert - Interaction with your present and future customer base is essential.
4. A Technology expert – It is must to know how technological changes in ANY industry would have on your business.

The best resource sites for businesses.

Moz - https://moz.com/

Jay Abraham - https://www.abraham.com/

Adobe - https://www.adobe.com/

TechCrunch - https://techcrunch.com/

GoToMeeting - https://www.gotomeeting.com/

Google Cloud - https://www.google.com/cloud/

HubSpot - https://blog.hubspot.com/

Brandwatch - https://www.brandwatch.com/

People to follow and listen to.

Some of these people are passed away already but there is enough materials, videos, books from them available that is worth looking at.

Jim Rohn

Stephen Richards Covey

Jay Abraham

Naveen Jain

Nicholas Kusmich

Peter Diamandis

Lisa Sasevich

Gary Vaynerchuk

Brian Tracy

Seth Godin

How the 80/20 rule applies to your company.

The 80/20 states 20% of something does 80% something.

20% of salespeople make 80% of sales.

20% of your products provide 80% of your income.

20% of your provide 80% of production –efficiency.

This rule applies to all part of your business. So take it in and see where and how you can use it.

BY THE WAY - just to make you look even more. Inside the 80/20 there is another 80/20. If you can examine your company that close you can really look at how you can improve, cut back, and grow.

Sales

Sales is the lifeblood of your company. Unfortunately, most companies do not know what to do with it.

Everything is sales. BIG SECRET: there is no such a thing B2B or B2C or any other sales!!!!!!

There is only P2P- Person to Person. (unless you are using bots) That means your people need to know how to talk to people.

90% of companies never do sales training. Also, let us get something straight. Learning communication skills, rejection techniques, and developing a very good sales technique is essential. But to make it to the highest level the mind has to be trained.

It has been proven that certain visualization techniques combined with mindfulness techniques provide a more exponential growth than just improving communication.

The first very good example of it was Bob Proctor teaching Prudential Life in the 80s. They implemented a very simple habit with mindfulness and visualization techniques. The company went from 200 Million/year to 3Billion/year in 2 or 3 years. There are other examples like that.

Customer Service

A lot of companies make the mistake that selling is customer service. Once I sold you thank you very much I am moving on.

It is, of course, short-sighted but in a lot of ways understandable for the salespeople whose only job is to sell you.

But here is where a lot of companies stop.

Selling a customer should be your first or second step in your relationship with them.

Costumer Service happens after you sell, and it is for people who already bought for you.

Let us also clear something else out. Marketing is for people who have not bought from you, and customer service is for people who already committed to your brand through a purchase.

Most companies do not understand this and tend to blur the lines between the two.

What this causes besides unhappy people is confusion in your expenses, because you cannot separate the finances properly.

By the way, customer service for your largest clients should be done by the CEO. Also, you do not just do it before the contract expires or when you want them to buy more. It should be a continuous relationship where appreciation is shown for the amount of money somebody spends with you.

After all, they are the ones keeping your company alive.

Fire prevention

Every large forest fire starts from a spark. So why do CEOs spend too much time putting fires out?

When you buy a machine – car- you have to perform maintenance on it. A machine is made of many moving parts and essential elements which without cannot work.

A company is like a car, many moving part, all of them essential for everything run smooth.

But if I would ask you if you are doing maintenance on your car, you would tell me that of course. So why not on your company.

I am in many executive forums, where every day I read about fire management and prioritizing which fire to put out first.

Brian Tracy said in one of his lectures, that companies – CEOs mostly only ask for help when the barn is on fire. He often asked the CEOs why not do preventative maintenance.

The answers boil down usually to these five things.

Pride, not knowing what do to, ego, too afraid to admit that he/she needs help, listening to people – management group that does not know what to do either.

I often see it with my wife´s clients. People with relationship problems giving advice to others having the same problems.

Like blind leading a blind.

There is no shame in admitting that you or your company needs help. Your, your workers, and your shareholders deserve that from you.

FIVE things a CEO must know when you hire them.

These are none specific order.

To start: What are the last 5 none textbooks were read by the person. Also, what are the last 3 business books he/she read in the past year?

1. Understanding of Finances. A CEO should have at least the basic understanding the flow of money in the organization. A lot of time decisions are made without any knowledge of the internal financial effects. Also when you know you are losing money, the understanding of what might and how it may cause it provides an easier way of fixing it.

2. Sales: The lifeblood of any company. You need to know how sales work, and how to sell. As a CEO if you want to know how to improve an area in the company or develop policies that will help a particular part of your company, you will need to know how that works. Since selling is your bloodline it is absolutely a most to understand.

3. Marketing. You give people a product to sell. You have to know how you can create a flow of continuous future customers/clients. You also have to know a must (99 out of 100 companies do not know) HOW MUCH you can spend on marketing. Almost all companies allocate. EVERY SINGLE DOLLAR allocated is wasted money.

4. Customer service: If you do not understand the people who bought your services or products already, you do not deserve to keep them. People come to you because you have something they need. It is your job to look after them. It is the biggest part of your business reputation building. Get this wrong and might as well close up the shop.

5. Internal communication skills: Would you believe that CEOs, in general, have more problem talking to their employees than to executives in other companies. It has been proven by many research that how interacting with employees by upper management including CEO has direct relations to the level of production.

Also, it is often viewed extremely positively when a CEO authentically brings a very positive and pleasant personality. The ability to positively interact with your employees is viewed as one of the most important areas the CEO masters.

Resume

Please put your hands up if you have a resume. The question is WHY? Okay, a better question is why companies still insisting on them.

When you are hiring a person why you are basing most of your decisions on a piece of paper or "digital information". After all, the paper is not going to work for you, but the person is.

A reality check. Anybody can put anything on a resume, and it is virtually impossible to know if it true or not. Do not start me with reference check. According to research, 96% information on a resume including references are never getting checked.

When I was 18 I was called by a company. They wanted to hire me but needed to check references. Guess what. It was summertime, none of them were reachable. They had to hire, so they never checked.

But why would we care to use an old outdated system where technology allows us so much flexibility.

When I ran my company we needed to hire, we asked people to submit a three-minute video, with their information. It worked extremely well for us. We used it as pre-interview. It cut our costs and time by a large amount.

I personally do not have a resume or any personal handout. When somebody wants to use my services, we connect.

It takes 5 to 10 minutes of talk (business and personal) to find out more about what somebody is all about and if they have the knowledge that is necessary. A resume could never give you that.

It is time for companies to realize that if they want to survive this decade and beyond they have to change how they used to conduct business. If not there are plenty of companies that are willing to take up the space you are leaving behind.

Try it. I guarantee you never go back.

Perspective

The biggest mistake a company can do is to hire a manager/executive from the same industry.

Why is that? Very simple. When you bring in a person who spent most of his/her time in the same area your company is, how much new insight can he/she bring? According to study about 15%.

When you look at any entity if it is creating a homogenous environment you can draw two conclusions. The quality of the outcome is going to be very similar over a longer period of time and that eventually it will become stagnated. This is why you see companies that used to dominate, disappear from relevance.

But the stagnated position does not necessarily come from the products they produce or at least not at first. It comes from thinking the same way on the top, leader after leader.

Companies when they are hiring WITHIN a company and within an industry without allowing any outside influence, these organizations tend to create homogenous environments.

When you are hiring a new manager/executive it is a must that you hire from a different industry. Here is the reason why. This person will bring a new perspective, new ideas – while he/she learns about your industry.

The new person will grow, and as he/she will grow so will your company.

Now do not take my word for this. But look at a person for me.

His name is Jay Abraham. If you have not heard of him – where have you been? His the defacto #1 marketing person on the planet. One of the reasons he is so effective is because he had been in dozens of industries.

When you have too much of the same all the time, growth will slow down and even stop.

CEO

Leaders come in many shapes and sizes. Make no mistake to be a CEO you have to be a leader.

As a CEO for almost 10 years, I discovered that everything in your company starts with you. If you cannot take that you should not be a CEO.

But how do you start? By looking at where you want to be, who you want to become, and to see where you are at the moment. To understand that the distance you need to cover can only be done by you, through learning about you, and after you know yourself better by learning more about business.

The process is not easy, but it is rewarding.

Seeing your company grow, seeing that you are able to give your family (your employees) the support that helps them to grow as people. Creating a mutually beneficial relationship with your suppliers, and to create an environment where your customers-clients take your brand to the next level, is what great CEOs aspire to achieve.

But all of this starts with you.

Growth

I have looked at a company because of personal interest in the past couple of days. I will not name it because it would not be fair to them.

This company a year ago (from information I was able to get) created an environment where they thought that they could double their output in an 11 month period. By the end of the year the situation crumple on them, and the CEO was let go.

Now a lot of you will disagree with me, but I am in a belief that large growth a lot of time is unsustainable and unhealthy. Unhealthy not because of your service or product, but what it does in the organization.

As a company, you have to make sure (dependent on your product and services) that the infrastructure is in place. That it is tested to make sure it can flex in case of rapid growth. If it is possible always use multiple lines, so in case one will falter you have another to use.

Here are some of the drawbacks that happen because of rapid growth: (depending on your industry)

Your vendors cannot handle extra capacity. Your vendors cannot produce the quality because of the volume. Breakdown of your machinery because of extra use. No way of fixing machinery because of no parts. More people have to be hired. Not sufficient time for training. More safety issues because of the extra people. Not enough time to screen people properly for personality issues. Insufficient packaging, storage area, equipment to move products around. Overtasked workers – more sick leave. Unexpected financial layout because of all of the above. …..and many other things.

You have to test your system many times and build in redundancy. You also always have to make sure that you are communicating with and getting the companies that you are relying on frontend and backend to be on board.

Just one example. When we needed a particular supplier on board, but they could not because they supplied other companies mainly our competition. Our other suppliers just could not handle that change. We ended up (it took almost 2 years) buying the supplier, and we were able to guarantee our supply.

Rapid growth has its glamour factor, but (depends on the industry, the product, and service) it brings with it a large amount possibilities of things going wrong. Steady smaller growth is always more advisable at least initially to make sure you create a base where growth is possible from.

Equality in the workplace.

The higher you go on the corporate food chain the less people see the effort on the bottom. I once heard one of my managers yell at the janitor because he left the floor to wet and he almost fell.

He said," Next time do a better job. You can be easily replaced. Anybody can do what you do."

The janitor put his head down, like a person who is afraid to say anything because he did not want to get fired.

I came out of the stall I looked at both of them. Both looked surprised but the manager even more.

I went to wash my hands, and both men used that opportunity to leave quietly.

I went outside the building because I felt that there was an aha moment there in that sentence. After walking (I do my best thinking when I am walking) I realized how little we appreciate what others do in a company. I realize that if this manager felt his way, how many other could have. Also how many people on the so-called lower levels would feel very negatively about what others do on the other levels of the corporate ladder.

So I initiated reverse work day, where managers had to be secretaries, cleaners, shippers, receivers, and warehouse workers for a day once every two weeks. Also the people they replaced experienced how it was on the higher levels.

The results were stunning. People got to a more mutually respected position about what everybody did.

I myself spent time on many levels. This gave me a better knowledge of the people working for me, but it also gave me a lot wider understanding how things worked in the company.

ONE big truth also came out all of it. Because I developed a lot closer relationship with people it was extremely difficult to even contemplate laying people off. It made you work harder as a CEO to make sure to take care of your people.

Authenticity

There is a rumor going around that now all the sudden to be a good leader you have to be authentic. What is to be authentic as a person or a leader is shrouded in many misunderstandings.

For many, it means to show your vulnerable side, and not being afraid to admit that you made a mistake.

To be honest looking at some people who are writing about authenticity it sort became a whine fest. Where all kinds of experiences from the past that these people considered bad are mentioned to nauseating levels.

And the only thing I can do is shake my hand. My advice to those who use this approach, think again.

Because to others, you would be nothing more than just a whiny baby.

Talking about how you were humiliated because in Blockbuster the women raised her voice at you when you forgot to rewind the tape and how traumatized you are because of that. Tell that to a woman who was just raped and you will see how much your so-called authenticity will carry you.

Can you imagine a CEO (mind you I have seen it when they are let go but not before) gets all the employees together for an announcement?

He says: I am so sorry I made a mistake. I went ahead invested our money in the wrong company. I did that even though I was told by everybody that it would be a bad idea. Yes, the bankruptcy sign on the door should have been a clue to me when I went to visit them. I am so very sorry, but you do not understand. When I was six I walked in on my mother and father doing it. You cannot imagine the horror. It scarred me for life. I cannot have a meaningful relationship even now as an adult.

Imagine what people going to think of you as you are wiping your dripping nose with your sleeve while you are crying like a baby.

If that is authenticity then might as well just break out the tissue box at all the CEO interviews. Because the person who had the most pathetic story and can cry like a baby will get the job from now on. They will be special classes on how to be authentic, where people are thought how to say sorry fifty different ways in twenty languages. Where they bring in actors just show you how to cry like a pro on cue.

You want to know how to be an effective CEO. As the CEO be true to yourself. That is authenticity. Care more about the people working for you than about yourself. Make the quality of your work just as important as the amount you want to get paid. Take care of your costumers better than your worry about your profit.

Your leadership should show knowledge, caring, compassion, and strength.

Leave the crying to Hollywood.

A me-centric universe.

Most people are living in a me-centric universe. That means when something happens in their environment the first thing they are asking is: What is the impact on me? This personal centric view is very natural and only a few people who are beyond it. Unfortunately, that is also the problem why so many businesses going belly up.

When you live in a me-centric universe, your life has its ups and downs. There is, however, more down than up. Most of the time life is not happy. You live in a disappointing, shallow, and often scary mental frame. The money will get you only so far, and you are constantly looking for things to fill the empty feeling of happiness.

Now imagine that the whole corporation is made of people just like that. How well will the business perform, and how well people will feel to work there on all levels.

On the basic level dealing with individuals whose life is generally speaking unhappy.

These individuals will think about themselves and talk to themselves on an unhappy level.

The workers on the lower level in this mental nightmare have to deal with and work with each other. You can see productivity, motivation, and caring toward beyond basics is very low on the priority. Money is not there as a motivating factor, and the fear of being let go at any time is a real fear that most people have at that level.

There is, of course, the upper management including executives (except CEO). Top of the food chain. Their job is to find ways to keep theirs. They are trying to plan out the big road ahead most of the time without knowing what exactly they are talking about.

The CEO. The loneliness position in a corporation voted almost five years running according to surveys in many business magazines. Imagine a lonely person, who has tremendous pressures on him or her to run a company profitably. They have no real feedback loop to help them analyze how well they are doing. Dealing with the board of directors that only care about stock prices nothing else.

The company has to leave the me-centered universe. The company has to create an environment where everybody (or close to it as physically possible) is more invested in doing well for the company and the customers than for themselves.

This change, however, has to come from the tip of the iceberg. The CEO. The CEO is the head of the corporation has to make a profound shift in the way of thinking, acting, talking, delegating and in realizing that your people are your priority. Helping your workers to achieve, to learn to become more than what they are, to guide them to figure out how to find happiness in their lives is the only way the corporation can change.

However first you as the CEO have to find all this in you.

A Teaching Guide

When you are the CEO, you are put on the pedestal of the hero. You are picked to save the day, and every day you are looked upon to do it again and again.

To the point when most CEOs believe that they are heroes instead of guides. This is where the underlying misunderstanding is when it comes to the role of the CEO.

First, let's clear something out. You the CEO as the person (Mark, Eva), yes you are the hero in your own life. You have to be. Because if you are not then you cannot achieve the success that you are capable of.

Your company cannot be the hero for your costumes. They have to be their own heroes as well.

However, like you to your company, your company to the costumers should be a guide and nothing more.

By the way, you will find that being a guide is more rewarding and allows more growth as well.

Of course for you to become the one that teaches not controls you have to make some fundamental changes in your personal life.

These changes might not be so easy because of the years you spent us a HERO. But when you realize how much reward comes with being the guide you will wonder how come you did not start earlier.

By the way, what is the difference between the Hero and the Guide?

The hero has the mission to solve a particular issue.

The guide is there to give - teach the hero whatever is necessary to solve the particular issue. However, it is up to the hero if it will or not.

More and more research shows that most growth happens when the internal feeling in the company matches the positive mindset of the individuals working there.

So if you do not have a positive mindset and the growth feeling inside your company you can imagine the growth you are missing.

As the CEO or leader of your company, the change has to come from you first.

Champion

If you look at any company see it in your mind like an iceberg. The tip that sticks out is everything you do physically inside your company. The bottom that you do not see, is all the displacement of mental focus, and effort that sinks you.

Imagine most of the companies constantly in the battle to try to fix the 10%, and mostly avoid the rest. You can increase sales, do better marketing, and or reduce expenses. It has been proven many times through research that the group thinking, mental image as a whole, and the belief of the people drive the company.

Don't believe me.

Look at any professional team. When it comes to skill the discrepancy is about ten percent, but the main driving force in performance is the mindset that drives the rest.

Let us look at FC Barcelona. Messi is a star, and you could agree or disagree that his skills are more than 10% above most.

However, when you listen to him, you realize that his determination his internal drive, and his internal view of himself as a champion that makes the difference. That is the same thing with Barcelona the club as well. Less than winning everything is frowned upon, and the whole organization looks at itself as the champion. You can feel that all the time.

When was the last time you felt that your company was the champion?

Thank you for reading.

The Quick of Guide of Awesomeness:

An easy way to jump-start your business or company.

ABOUT THE AUTHOR

Gabriel Ronkai America´s Financial Efficiency Expert - CEO, and successful entrepreneur.

He has helped companies around the world as The Virtual CEO.

www.ingramcontent.com/pod-product-compliance
Lightning Source LLC
Chambersburg PA
CBHW062237220526
45471CB00009B/3527